TRIFLES

SUSAN GLASPELL

ISBN: 978-1494891220

Introduction

Susan Glaspell's one act play, *Trifles*, was first performed in 1916 and published in the same year. Glaspell grew up in the Mid-West, but moved to Provincetown in Cape Cod when she got married. She was a member of an élite amateur acting group – the Provincetown Players – who staged many of her early plays. The events of the play are said to be based on a crime that occurred in Des Moines and which she reported for the local newspaper when she worked as a journalist before moving east. Trifles seems to be set in the Mid-West, but it could be set anywhere in rural America.

The main character in *Trifles* is arguably one who never appears on stage – Mrs. Wright – who is in police custody after her husband was found dead with a noose around his head; although he is dead, Mr. Wright is also an important character, and what we learn during the play about the Wrights' marriage is crucial to an understanding of what happened and why, and an appreciation of Glaspell's larger concerns.

The play itself consists of a visit by the County Attorney and the Sheriff who visit the Wright house in an attempt to find evidence of what they assume is a murder. Mrs. Wright claims not to have heard anything in the night and to know nothing about her husband's death. The Country Attorney and the Sheriff are accompanied by Hale, a neighbor of the Wrights' and husband to one of the women who is also on stage There are two women on stage: Mrs. Peters, the wife of the Sheriff, and Mrs. Hale who is a close neighbor of the Wrights.

The main conflict in the play is between the male and the female characters. The male characters have come to find evidence that will prove that Mrs. Wright killed her husband; the female characters are there to defend the absent Mrs. Wright in a demonstration of female solidarity. For example, when surveying the untidy and messy kitchen, the County Attorney remarks of Mrs. Wright, "Not much of a housekeeper, would you say, ladies?" However, Mrs Hale replies, "There's a great deal of work to be done on a farm". The men's attitude to women in general is patronizing and belittling. When it is revealed that Mrs. Wright is worried that her jars of preserves in a cold house would freeze, Hale remarks, "women are used to worrying over trifles." As the County Attorney continues with his questions, it becomes clear that the Wright household was not a happy place. Mrs.

Hale has not been inside the house for more than a year, because, she says, "It never seemed a very cheerful place". The County Attorney remarks that its lack of cheerfulness must be due to Mrs. Wright's lack of "the home-making instinct", but Mrs. Hale retorts that Mr. Wright was as much to blame: "I don't think a place'd be any cheerfuller for John Wright being in it". This makes it clear to the audience that some animosity existed between Mr. and Mrs. Wright.

The men go upstairs to inspect the bed where Wright died, leaving the women alone in the kitchen. Mrs. Hale and Mrs. Peters look around the kitchen, and they notice tiny signs that Mrs. Wright was planning for the future – she was making a quilt – and they have also come to gather things that she has asked to be taken to her in prison. Their conversation reveals more about the dead man and his imprisoned wife. When Mrs. Peters remarks on how cold the house is, Mrs. Hale asserts, "Wright was close" – in other words, he was mean and would not spend money on adequate heating. They also reminisce about how lively and spirited Mrs. Wright was before she was married: "She used to wear pretty clothes and be lively, when she was Minnie Foster". The women remark that as far as the men are concerned it is a simple case: Mrs. Wright murdered her husband – they simply have to find the evidence. They then notice an empty bird cage, and recall Mrs. Wright's love of singing. Mrs. Hale makes the comparison explicit: "She was kind of like a bird herself – real sweet and pretty, but kind of timid and – fluttery". Then they find the dead bird: it neck has been wrung, and suddenly the whole story becomes clear to the audience. Mr. Wright killed his wife's canary – the only thing of joy and pleasure in her life and, in revenge, she killed him. Ironically, the women, who have been in the kitchen preoccupied with things the men would call "trifles", have arrived at the truth. After thirty years of marriage to a hard. Tight-fisted man, and with nothing to call her own, Mrs. Wright has finally rebelled and murdered her husband. His killing of her pet bird was the final thing that drove her to this act of desperation. At the end of play the County Attorney says, "It's all perfectly clear except a reason for doing it". This is deeply ironic because Mrs. Peters, Mrs. Hale and the audience know exactly why Mrs. Wright killed her joyless husband.

The climax of the play is the discovery of the murdered bird. The conflict throughout the play is between the genders. The men keep searching for evidence in a business-like way and dismissing the women's concern with trivial things – the 'trifles' of the title. But Glaspell uses irony to show that because the women can sympathize and empathize with Mrs. Wright, they are able to arrive at the truth. The mood overall is one of melancholy and sadness, which is provoked by the knowledge that Mrs. Wright will be found guilty of murder and also sadness at the empty and unhappy life she has led with her husband. When the male characters are on stage, the mood lightens – simply because they do not understand what has really happened in the Wright household.

Trifles, in a very concise way, raises important themes about gender stereotypes, and showed how oppressive it is for women to live in a patriarchal society. It is good literature – partly because of its brevity, and its slow revelation of the truth; Glaspell's use of irony is clever and the play raises some issues which are as relevant today as they were in 1916. Glaspell's intention in writing the play was surely to present a patriarchal society in a bad light, and to draw attention both to gender stereotyping and the many women trapped in unhappy, loveless marriages.

SCENE. The kitchen in the now abandoned farmhouse of John Wright, a gloomy kitchen, and left without having been put in order--unwashed pans under the sink, a loaf of bread outside the bread-box, a dish-towel on the table--other signs of incompleted work. At the rear the outer door opens and the Sheriff comes in followed by the County Attorney and Hale. The Sheriff and Hale are in middle life, the County Attorney is a young man; all are much bundled up and go at once to the stove. They are followed by the two women--the Sheriff's wife first; she is a slight wiry woman, a thin nervous face. Mrs. Hale is larger and would ordinarily be called more comfortable looking, but she is disturbed now and looks fearfully about as she enters. The women have come in slowly, and stand close together near the door.

COUNTY ATTORNEY [*Rubbing his hands.*] This feels good. Come up to the fire, ladies.

MRS. PETERS [*After taking a step forward.*] I'm not--cold.

SHERIFF [*Unbuttoning his overcoat and stepping away from the stove as if to mark the beginning of official business.*] Now, Mr. Hale, before we move things about, you explain to Mr. Henderson just what you saw when you came here yesterday morning.

COUNTY ATTORNEY By the way, has anything been moved? Are things just as you left them yesterday?

SHERIFF [*Looking about.*] It's just the same. When it dropped below zero last night I thought I'd better send Frank out this morning to make a fire for us--no use getting pneumonia with a big case on, but I told him not to touch anything except the stove--and you know Frank.

COUNTY ATTORNEY Somebody should have been left here yesterday.

SHERIFF Oh--yesterday. When I had to send Frank to Morris Center for that man who went crazy--I want you to know I had my hands full yesterday. I knew you could get back from Omaha by today and as long as I went over everything here myself--

COUNTY ATTORNEY Well, Mr. Hale, tell just what happened when you came here yesterday morning.

HALE Harry and I had started to town with a load of potatoes. We came along the road from my place and as I got here I said, "I'm going to see if I can't get John Wright to go in with me on a party telephone." I spoke to Wright about it once before and he put me off, saying folks talked too much anyway, and all he asked was peace and quiet--I guess you know about how much he talked himself, but I thought maybe if I went to the house and talked about it before his wife, though I said to Harry that I didn't know as what his wife wanted made much difference to John--

COUNTY ATTORNEY Let's talk about that later, Mr. Hale. I do want to talk about that, but tell now just what happened when you got to the house.

HALE I didn't hear or see anything; I knocked at the door, and still it was all quiet inside. I knew they must be up, it was past eight o'clock. So I knocked again, and I thought I heard somebody say, "Come in." I wasn't sure, I'm not sure yet, but I opened the door--this door [*indicating the door by which the two women are still standing*] and there in that rocker--[*pointing to it*] sat Mrs. Wright.

[*They all look at the rocker.*]

COUNTY ATTORNEY What--was she doing?

HALE She was rockin' back and forth. She had her apron in her hand and was kind of--pleating it.

COUNTY ATTORNEY And how did she--look?

HALE Well, she looked queer.

COUNTY ATTORNEY How do you mean--queer?

HALE Well, as if she didn't know what she was going to do next. And kind of done up.

COUNTY ATTORNEY How did she seem to feel about your coming?

HALE Why, I don't think she minded--one way or other. She didn't pay much attention. I said, "How do, Mrs. Wright, it's cold, ain't it?" And she said, "Is it?"--and went on kind of pleating at her apron. Well, I was surprised; she didn't ask me to come up to the stove, or to set down, but just sat there, not even looking at me, so I said, "I want to see John." And then she--laughed, I guess you would call it a laugh. I thought of Harry and the team outside, so I said a little sharp: "Can't I see John?" "No," she says, kind o' dull like. "Ain't he home?" says I. "Yes," says she, "he's home." "Then why can't I see him?" I asked her, out of patience. "'Cause he's dead," says she. "*Dead?*" says I. She just nodded her head, not getting a bit excited, but rockin' back and forth. "Why-- where is he?" says I, not knowing what to say. She just pointed upstairs--like that [*himself pointing to the room above*]. I got up, with the idea of going up there. I walked from there to here--then I says, "Why, what did he die of?" "He died of a rope round his neck," says she, and just went on pleatin' at her apron. Well, I went out and called Harry. I thought I might--need help. We went upstairs and there he was lyin'--

COUNTY ATTORNEY I think I'd rather have you go into that upstairs, where you can point it all out. Just go on now with the rest of the story.

HALE Well, my first thought was to get that rope off. It looked . . . [*Stops, his face twitches*] . . . but Harry, he went up to him, and he said, "No, he's dead all right, and we'd better not touch anything." So we went back downstairs. She was still sitting that same way. "Has anybody been notified?" I asked. "No," says she, unconcerned. "Who did this, Mrs. Wright?" said Harry. He said it business-like--and she stopped pleatin' of her apron. "I don't know," she says. "You don't *know*?" says Harry. "No," says she. "Weren't you sleepin' in the bed with him?" says Harry. "Yes," says she, "but I was on the inside." "Somebody slipped a rope round his neck and strangled him and you didn't wake up?" says Harry. "I didn't wake up," she said after him. We must 'a looked as if we didn't see how that could be, for after a minute she said, "I sleep sound." Harry was going to ask her more questions but I said maybe we ought to let her tell her story first to the coroner, or the sheriff, so Harry went fast as he could to Rivers' place, where there's a telephone.

COUNTY ATTORNEY And what did Mrs. Wright do when she knew that you had gone for the coroner?

HALE She moved from that chair to this one over here [*Pointing to a small chair in the corner*] and just sat there with her hands held together and looking down. I got a feeling that I ought to make some conversation, so I said I had come in to see if John wanted to put in a telephone, and at that she started to laugh, and then she stopped and looked at me--scared. [*The County Attorney, who has had his note book out, makes a note.*] I dunno, maybe it wasn't scared. I wouldn't like to say it was. Soon Harry got back, and then

Dr. Lloyd came, and you, Mr. Peters, and so I guess that's all I know that you don't.

COUNTY ATTORNEY [*Looking around.*] I guess we'll go upstairs first--and then out to the barn and around there. [*To the Sheriff.*] You're convinced that there was nothing important here--nothing that would point to any motive.

SHERIFF Nothing here but kitchen things.

[*The County Attorney, after again looking around the kitchen, opens the door of a cupboard closet. He gets up on a chair and looks on a shelf. Pulls his hand away, sticky.*

COUNTY ATTORNEY Here's a nice mess.

[*The women draw nearer.*

PETERS [*To the other woman.*] Oh, her fruit; it did freeze. [*To the Lawyer.*] She worried about that when it turned so cold. She said the fire'd go out and her jars would break.

SHERIFF Well, can you beat the women! Held for murder and worryin' about her preserves.

COUNTY ATTORNEY I guess before we're through she may have something more serious than preserves to worry about.

HALE Well, women are used to worrying over trifles.

[*The two women move a little closer together.*

COUNTY ATTORNEY [*With the gallantry of a young politician.*] And yet, for all their worries, what would we do without the ladies? [*The women do not unbend. He goes to the sink, takes a dipperful of water from the pail and pouring it into a basin, washes his hands. Starts to wipe them on the roller-towel, turns it for a cleaner place.*] Dirty towels!

[*Kicks his foot against the pans under the sink.*] Not much of a housekeeper, would you say, ladies?

MRS. HALE [*Stiffly.*] There's a great deal of work to be done on a farm.

COUNTY ATTORNEY To be sure. And yet [*With a little bow to her*] I know there are some Dickson county farmhouses which do not have such roller towels.

[He gives it a pull to expose its full length again.

MRS. HALE Those towels get dirty awful quick. Men's hands aren't always as clean as they might be.

COUNTY ATTORNEY Ah, loyal to your sex, I see. But you and Mrs. Wright were neighbors. I suppose you were friends, too.

MRS. HALE [*Shaking her head.*] I've not seen much of her of late years. I've not been in this house--it's more than a year.

COUNTY ATTORNEY And why was that? You didn't like her?

MRS. HALE I liked her all well enough. Farmers' wives have their hands full, Mr. Henderson. And then--

COUNTY ATTORNEY Yes--?

MRS. HALE [*Looking about.*] It never seemed a very cheerful place.

COUNTY ATTORNEY No--it's not cheerful. I shouldn't say she had the homemaking instinct.

MRS. HALE Well, I don't know as Wright had, either.

COUNTY ATTORNEY You mean that they didn't get on very well?

MRS. HALE No, I don't mean anything. But I don't think a place'd be any cheerfuller for John Wright's being in it.

COUNTY ATTORNEY I'd like to talk more of that a little later. I want to get the lay of things upstairs now.

[He goes to the left, where three steps lead to a stair door.

SHERIFF I Suppose anything Mrs. Peters does'll be all right. She was to take in some clothes for her, you know, and a few little things. We left in such a hurry yesterday.

COUNTY ATTORNEY Yes, but I would like to see what you take, Mrs. Peters, and keep an eye out for anything that might be of use to us.

MRS. PETERS Yes, Mr. Henderson.

[The women listen to the men's steps on the stairs, then look about the kitchen.

MRS. HALE I'd hate to have men coming into my kitchen, snooping around and criticising.

[She arranges the pans under sink which the Lawyer had shoved out of place.

MRS. PETERS Of course it's no more than their duty.

MRS. HALE Duty's all right, but I guess that deputy sheriff that came out to make the fire might have got a little of this on. [*Gives the roller towel a pull.*] Wish I'd thought of that sooner. Seems mean to talk about her for not having things slicked up when she had to come away in such a hurry.

MRS. PETERS [*Who has gone to a small table in the left rear corner of the room, and lifted one end of a towel that covers a pan.*] She had bread set.

[*Stands still.*

MRS. HALE [*Eyes fixed on a loaf of bread beside the breadbox, which is on a low shelf at the other side of the room. Moves slowly toward it.*] She was going to put this in there. [*Picks up loaf, then abruptly drops it. In a manner of returning to familiar things.*] It's a shame about her fruit. I wonder if it's all gone. [*Gets up on the chair and looks.*] I think there's some here that's all right, Mrs. Peters. Yes-- here; [*Holding it toward the window*] this is cherries, too. [*Looking again.*] I declare I believe that's the only one. [*Gets down, bottle in her hand. Goes to the sink and wipes it off on the outside.*] She'll feel awful bad after all her hard work in the hot weather. I remember the afternoon I put up my cherries last summer.

[*She puts the bottle on the big kitchen table, center of the room. With a sigh, is about to sit down in the rocking-chair. Before she is seated realizes what chair it is; with a slow look at it, steps back. The chair which she has touched rocks back and forth.*

MRS. PETERS Well, I must get those things from the front room closet. [*She goes to the door at the right, but after looking into the other room, steps back.*] You coming with me, Mrs. Hale? You could help me carry them.

[*They go in the other room; reappear, Mrs. Peters carrying a dress and skirt, Mrs. Hale following with a pair of shoes.*

MRS. PETERS My, it's cold in there.

[*She puts the clothes on the big table, and hurries to the stove.*

MRS. HALE [*Examining the skirt.*] Wright was close. I think maybe that's why she kept so much to herself. She didn't even belong to the Ladies Aid. I suppose she felt she couldn't do her part, and then you don't enjoy things when you feel shabby. She used to wear pretty clothes and be lively, when she was Minnie Foster, one of the town girls singing in the choir. But that--oh, that was thirty years ago. This all you was to take in?

MRS. PETERS She said she wanted an apron. Funny thing to want, for there isn't much to get you dirty in jail, goodness knows. But I suppose just to make her feel more natural. She said they was in the top drawer in this cupboard. Yes, here. And then her little shawl that always hung behind the door. [*Opens stair door and looks.*] Yes, here it is.

[*Quickly shuts door leading upstairs.*

MRS. HALE [*Abruptly moving toward her.*] Mrs. Peters?

MRS. PETERS Yes, Mrs. Hale?

MRS. HALE Do you think she did it?

MRS. PETERS [*In a frightened voice.*] Oh, I don't know.

MRS. HALE Well, I don't think she did. Asking for an apron and her little shawl. Worrying about her fruit.

MRS. PETERS [*Starts to speak, glances up, where footsteps are heard in the room above. In a low voice.*] Mr. Peters says it looks bad for her. Mr. Henderson is awful sarcastic in a speech and he'll make fun of her sayin' she didn't wake up.

MRS. HALE Well, I guess John Wright didn't wake when they was slipping that rope under his neck.

MRS. PETERS No, it's strange. It must have been done awful crafty and still. They say it was such a--funny way to kill a man, rigging it all up like that.

MRS. HALE That's just what Mr. Hale said. There was a gun in the house. He says that's what he can't understand.

MRS. PETERS Mr. Henderson said coming out that what was needed for the case was a motive; something to show anger, or--sudden feeling.

MRS. HALE [*Who is standing by the table.*] Well, I don't see any signs of anger around here. [*She puts her hand on the dish towel which lies on the table, stands looking down at table, one half of which is clean, the other half messy.*] It's wiped to here. [*Makes a move as if to finish work, then turns and looks at loaf of bread outside the breadbox. Drops towel. In that voice of coming back to familiar things.*] Wonder how they are finding things upstairs. I hope she had it a little more red-up up there. You know, it seems kind of sneaking. Locking her up in town and then coming out here and trying to get her own house to turn against her!

MRS. PETERS But Mrs. Hale, the law is the law.

MRS. HALE I s'pose 'tis. [*Unbuttoning her coat.*] Better loosen up your things, Mrs. Peters. You won't feel them when you go out.

[*Mrs. Peters takes off her fur tippet, goes to hang it on hook at back of room, stands looking at the under part of the small corner table.*

MRS. PETERS She was piecing a quilt.

[*She brings the large serving basket and they look at the bright pieces.*

MRS. HALE It's log-cabin pattern. Pretty, isn't it? I wonder if she was goin' to quilt it or just knot it?

[Footsteps have been heard coming down the stairs. The Sheriff enters followed by Hale and the County Attorney.

SHERIFF They wonder if she was going to quilt it or just knot it!

[The men laugh, the women look abashed.

COUNTY ATTORNEY *[Rubbing his hands over the stove.]* Frank's fire didn't do much up there, did it? Well, let's go out to the barn and get that cleared up.

[The men go outside.

MRS. HALE *[Resentfully.]* I don't know as there's anything so strange, our takin' up our time with little things while we're waiting for them to get the evidence. *[She sits down at the big table smoothing out a block with decision.]* I don't see as it's anything to laugh about.

MRS. PETERS *[Apologetically.]* Of course they've got awful important things on their minds.

[Pulls up a chair and joins Mrs. Hale at the table.

MRS. HALE *[Examining another block.]* Mrs. Peters, look at this one. Here, this is the one she was working on, and look at the sewing! All the rest of it has been so nice and even. And look at this! It's all over the place! Why, it looks as if she didn't know what she was about!

[After she had said this they look at each other, then start to glance back at the door. After an instant Mrs. Hale has pulled at a knot and ripped the sewing.

MRS. PETERS Oh, what are you doing, Mrs. Hale?

MRS. HALE [*Mildly.*] Just pulling out a stitch or two that's not sewed very good. [*Threading a needle.*] Bad sewing always made me fidgety.

MRS. PETERS [*Nervously.*] I don't think we ought to touch things.

MRS. HALE I'll just finish up this end. [*Suddenly stopping and leaning forward.*] Mrs. Peters?

MRS. PETERS Yes, Mrs. Hale?

MRS. HALE What do you suppose she was so nervous about?

MRS. PETERS Oh--I don't know. I don't know as she was nervous. I sometimes sew awful queer when I'm just tired. [*Mrs. Hale starts to say something, looks at Mrs. Peters, then goes on sewing.*] Well I must get these things wrapped up. They may be through sooner than we think. [*Putting apron and other things together.*] I wonder where I can find a piece of paper, and string.

MRS. HALE In that cupboard, maybe.

MRS. PETERS [*Looking in cupboard.*] Why, here's a bird-cage. [*Holds it up.*] Did she have a bird, Mrs. Hale?

MRS. HALE Why, I don't know whether she did or not--I've not been here for so long. There was a man around last year selling canaries cheap, but I don't know as she took one; maybe she did. She used to sing real pretty herself.

MRS. PETERS [*Glancing around.*] Seems funny to think of a bird here. But she must have had one, or why would she have a cage? I wonder what happened to it.

MRS. HALE I s'pose maybe the cat got it.

MRS. PETERS No, she didn't have a cat. She's got that feeling some people have about cats--being afraid of them. My cat got in her room and she was real upset and asked me to take it out.

MRS. HALE My sister Bessie was like that. Queer, ain't it?

MRS. PETERS [*Examining the cage.*] Why, look at this door. It's broke. One hinge is pulled apart.

MRS. HALE [*Looking too.*] Looks as if someone must have been rough with it.

MRS. PETERS Why, yes.

[*She brings the cage forward and puts it on the table.*

MRS. HALE I wish if they're going to find any evidence they'd be about it. I don't like this place.

MRS. PETERS But I'm awful glad you came with me, Mrs. Hale. It would be lonesome for me sitting here alone.

MRS. HALE It would, wouldn't it? [*Dropping her sewing.*] But I tell you what I do wish, Mrs. Peters. I wish I had come over sometimes when she was here. I-- [*Looking around the room*]--wish I had.

MRS. PETERS But of course you were awful busy, Mrs. Hale--your house and your children.
MRS. HALE I could've come. I stayed away because it weren't cheerful--and that's why I ought to have come. I--I've never liked this place. Maybe because it's down in a hollow and you don't see the road. I dunno what it is, but it's a lonesome place and always was, I wish I had come over to see Minnie Foster sometimes. I can see now--

[*Shakes her head.*

MRS. PETERS Well, you mustn't reproach yourself, Mrs. Hale. Somehow we just don't see how it is with other folks until--something comes up.

MRS. HALE Not having children makes less work--but it makes a quiet house, and Wright out to work all day, and no company when he did come in. Did you know John Wright, Mrs. Peters?

MRS. PETERS No; I've seen him in town. They say he was a good man.

MRS. HALE Yes--good; he didn't drink, and kept his word as well as most, I guess, and paid his debts. But he was a hard man, Mrs. Peters. Just to pass the time of day with him-- [*Shivers.*] Like a raw wind that gets to the bone. [*Pauses, her eye falling on the cage.*] I should think she would 'a wanted a bird. But what do you suppose went with it?

MRS. PETERS I don't know, unless it got sick and died.

[*She reaches over and swings the broken door, swings it again, both women watch it.*

MRS. HALE You weren't raised round here, were you? [*Mrs. Peters shakes her head.*] You didn't know--her?

MRS. PETERS Not till they brought her yesterday.

MRS. HALE She--come to think of it, she was kind of like a bird herself--real sweet and pretty, but kind of timid and--fluttery. How--she--did--change. [*Silence; then as if struck by a happy thought and relieved to get back to every day things.*] Tell you what, Mrs. Peters, why don't you take the quilt in with you? It might take up her mind.

MRS. PETERS Why, I think that's a real nice idea, Mrs. Hale. There couldn't possibly be any objection to it, could there? Now, just what would I take? I wonder if her patches are in here--and her things.

[*They look in the sewing basket.*

MRS. HALE Here's some red. I expect this has got sewing things in it. [*Brings out a fancy box.*] What a pretty box. Looks like something somebody would give you. Maybe her scissors are in here. [*Opens box. Suddenly puts her hand to her nose.*] Why-- [*Mrs. Peters bends nearer, then turns her face away.*] There's something wrapped up in this piece of silk.

MRS. PETERS Why, this isn't her scissors.

MRS. HALE [*Lifting the silk.*] Oh, Mrs. Peters--its--

[*Mrs. Peters bends closer.*

MRS. PETERS It's the bird.

MRS. HALE [*Jumping up.*] But, Mrs. Peters--look at it! Its neck! Look at its neck! It's all--to the other side.

MRS. PETERS Somebody--wrung--its--neck.

[*Their eyes meet. A look of growing comprehension, of horror. Steps are heard outside. Mrs. Hale slips box under quilt pieces, and sinks into her chair. Enter Sheriff and County Attorney. Mrs. Peters rises.*

COUNTY ATTORNEY [*As one turning from serious things to little pleasantries.*] Well, ladies, have you decided whether she was going to quilt it or knot it?

MRS. PETERS We think she was going to--knot it.

COUNTY ATTORNEY Well, that's interesting, I'm sure. [*Seeing the birdcage.*] Has the bird flown?

MRS. HALE [*Putting more quilt pieces over the box.*] We think the--cat got it.

COUNTY ATTORNEY [*Preoccupied.*] Is there a cat?

[*Mrs. Hale glances in a quick covert way at Mrs. Peters.*

MRS. PETERS Well, not now. They're superstitious, you know. They leave.

COUNTY ATTORNEY [*To Sheriff Peters, continuing an interrupted conversation.*] No sign at all of anyone having come from the outside. Their own rope. Now let's go up again and go over it piece by piece. [*They start upstairs.*] It would have to have been someone who knew just the--

[*Mrs. Peters sits down. The two women sit there not looking at one another, but as if peering into something and at the same time holding back. When they talk now it is in the manner of feeling their way over strange ground, as if afraid of what they are saying, but as if they cannot help saying it.*

MRS. HALE She liked the bird. She was going to bury it in that pretty box.

MRS. PETERS [*In a whisper*] When I was a girl--my kitten-- there was a boy took a hatchet, and before my eyes--and before I could get there--[*Covers her face an instant.*] If they hadn't held me back I would have--[*Catches herself, looks upstairs where steps are heard, falters weakly*]--hurt him.

MRS. HALE [*With a slow look around her.*] I wonder how it would seem never to have had any children around. [*Pause.*] No, Wright wouldn't like the bird--a thing that sang. She used to sing. He killed that, too.

MRS. PETERS [*Moving uneasily.*] We don't know who killed the bird.

MRS. HALE I knew John Wright.

MRS. PETERS It was an awful thing was done in this house that night, Mrs. Hale. Killing a man while he slept, slipping a rope around his neck that choked the life out of him.

MRS. HALE His neck. Choked the life out of him.

[Her hand goes out and rests on the bird-cage.

MRS. PETERS [*With rising voice.*] We don't know who killed him. We don't *know*.

MRS. HALE [*Her own feeling not interrupted.*] If there'd been years and years of nothing, then a bird to sing to you, it would be awful--still, after the bird was still.

MRS. PETERS [*Something within her speaking.*] I know what stillness is. When we homesteaded in Dakota, and my first baby died--after he was two years old, and me with no other then--

MRS. HALE [*Moving.*] How soon do you suppose they'll be through, looking for the evidence?

MRS. PETERS I know what stillness is. [*Pulling herself back.*] The law has got to punish crime, Mrs. Hale.

MRS. HALE [*Not as if answering that.*] I wish you'd seen Minnie Foster when she wore a white dress with blue ribbons and stood up there in the choir and sang. [*A look around the room.*] Oh, I wish I'd come over here once in a while! That was a crime! That was a crime! Who's going to punish that?

MRS. PETERS [*Looking upstairs.*] We mustn't--take on.

MRS. HALE I might have known she needed help! I know how things can be--for women, I tell you, it's queer, Mrs. Peters. We live close together and we live far apart. We all go through the same things--it's all just a different kind of the same thing. [*Brushes her eyes, noticing the bottle of fruit, reaches out for it.*] If I was you I wouldn't tell her her fruit was gone. Tell her it ain't. Tell her it's all right. Take this in to prove it to her. She--she may never know whether it was broke or not.

MRS. PETERS [*Takes the bottle, looks about for something to wrap it in; takes petticoat from the clothes brought from the other room, very nervously begins winding this around the bottle. In a false voice.*] My, it's a good thing the men couldn't hear us. Wouldn't they just laugh! Getting all stirred up over a little thing like a--dead canary. As if that could have anything to do with--with--wouldn't they *laugh!*

[*The men are heard coming down stairs.*

MRS. HALE [*Under her breath.*] Maybe they would--maybe they wouldn't.

COUNTY ATTORNEY No, Peters, it's all perfectly clear except a reason for doing it. But you know juries when it comes to women. If there was some definite thing. Something to show--something to make a story about--a thing that would connect up with this strange way of doing it--

[*The women's eyes meet for an instant. Enter Hale from outer door.*

HALE Well, I've got the team around. Pretty cold out there.

COUNTY ATTORNEY I'm going stay here a while by myself. [*To the Sheriff.*] You can send Frank out for me, can't you? I want to go over everything. I'm not satisfied that we can't do better.

SHERIFF Do you want to see what Mrs. Peters is going to take in?

[*The Lawyer goes to the table, picks up the apron, laughs.*

COUNTY ATTORNEY Oh, I guess they're not very dangerous things the ladies have picked out. [*Moves a few things about, disturbing the quilt pieces which cover the box. Steps back.*] No, Mrs. Peters doesn't need supervising. For that matter, a sheriff's wife is married to the law. Ever think of it that way, Mrs. Peters?

MRS. PETERS Not--just that way.

SHERIFF [*Chuckling.*] Married to the law. [*Moves toward the other room.*] I just want you to come in here a minute, George. We ought to take a look at these windows.

COUNTY ATTORNEY [*Scoffingly.*] Oh, windows!

SHERIFF We'll be right out, Mr. Hale.

[*Hale goes outside. The Sheriff follows the County Attorney into the other room. Then Mrs. Hale rises, hands tight together, looking intensely at Mrs. Peters, whose eyes make a slow turn, finally meeting Mrs. Hale's. A moment Mrs. Hale holds her, then her own eyes point the way to where the box is concealed. Suddenly Mrs. Peters throws back quilt pieces and tries to put the box in the bag she is wearing. It is too big. She opens box, starts to take bird out, cannot touch it, goes to pieces, stands there helpless. Sound of a knob turning in the other room. Mrs. Hale snatches the box and puts it in the pocket of her big coat. Enter County Attorney and Sheriff.*

COUNTY ATTORNEY [*Facetiously.*] Well, Henry, at least we found out that she was not going to quilt it. She was going to--what is it you call it, ladies?

MRS. HALE [*Her hand against her pocket.*] We call it--<u>knot</u> <u>it</u>, Mr. Henderson.

(CURTAIN)

Made in the USA
Las Vegas, NV
13 February 2023